Garfield's

Guide
To
CAT NAPPING

D1638905

JIM DAVIS

RAVETTE PUBLISHING

This edition first published by Ravette Publishing Limited in 2001.

Printed and bound for Ravette Publishing Limited
Unit 3, Tristar Centre
Star Road, Partridge Green
West Sussex RH13 8RA

by Gutenberg Press Ltd, Malta.

ISBN: 1 84161 087 9

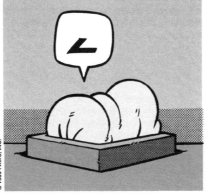

UH... GARFIELD...

BECAUSE NAP ATTACKS CAN STRIKE ANYTIME, ANYWHERE, WITHOUT WARNING, THAT'S WHY

JIM DAVIS 4-15

JIM DAVIS 4-16

JIM DAVIS 11-3

JIM DAVIS 11-4